THIS
WALKING & HIKING IN IRELAND

2 IN 1

JOURNAL / NOTEBOOK

BELONGS TO

Name ....

E MAIL ....

MOBILE ....

BLOG ....

PLEASE RETURN IF FOUND

WALKING & HIKING IN IRELAND JOURNAL

TODAY'S DATE .... / ..../ ....

START LOCATION GPS ....

START LOCATION / ADDRESS

....
....
....

POST CODE .... PLANNED DISTANCE...............
TODAY'S WEATHER ....
TODAY'S TEMPERATURE .... START TIME ....
TODAY'S COMPANIONS ....
TODAY'S COMPANIONS ....
TODAY'S COMPANIONS ....
TODAY'S COMPANIONS ....
BREAKFAST ....
LUNCH ....
DINNER ....
WILDLIFE SEEN ....
END TIME .... TIME TAKEN ....
MILES COVERED .... DIFFICULTY 1 2 3 4 5
HIKE RATING ☆ ☆ ☆ ☆ ☆

TODAY'S HIGHLIGHTS

....
....
....
....

WALKING & HIKING NOTES

WALKING & HIKING IN IRELAND JOURNAL

TODAY'S DATE ..../..../........

START LOCATION GPS ....

START LOCATION / ADDRESS

....
....
....

POST CODE .... PLANNED DISTANCE................

TODAY'S WEATHER ....

TODAY'S TEMPERATURE .... START TIME ....

TODAY'S COMPANIONS ....

TODAY'S COMPANIONS ....

TODAY'S COMPANIONS ....

TODAY'S COMPANIONS ....

BREAKFAST ....

LUNCH ....

DINNER ....

WILDLIFE SEEN ....

END TIME .... TIME TAKEN ....

MILES COVERED .... DIFFICULTY 1 2 3 4 5

HIKE RATING ☆ ☆ ☆ ☆ ☆ ☆

TODAY'S HIGHLIGHTS

....
....
....
....

WALKING / HIKING NOTES

WALKING & HIKING IN IRELAND JOURNAL

TODAY'S DATE …. / …./ ……..

START LOCATION GPS ……………………………………………

START LOCATION / ADDRESS

……………………………………………………………………
……………………………………………………………………
……………………………………………………………………

POST CODE ………………… PLANNED DISTANCE……………

TODAY'S WEATHER ……………………………………………

TODAY'S TEMPERATURE ……………… START TIME …………

TODAY'S COMPANIONS …………………………………………

TODAY'S COMPANIONS …………………………………………

TODAY'S COMPANIONS …………………………………………

TODAY'S COMPANIONS …………………………………………

BREAKFAST ………………………………………………………

LUNCH ……………………………………………………………

DINNER ……………………………………………………………

WILDLIFE SEEN …………………………………………………

END TIME ………………… TIME TAKEN …………………

MILES COVERED …………… DIFFICULTY 1 2 3 4 5

HIKE RATING ☆ ☆ ☆ ☆ ☆ ☆

TODAY'S HIGHLIGHTS

……………………………………………………………………
……………………………………………………………………
……………………………………………………………………
……………………………………………………………………

WALKING / HIKING NOTES

WALKING & HIKING IN IRELAND JOURNAL

TODAY'S DATE .... / .... / ....

START LOCATION GPS ....

START LOCATION / ADDRESS

....
....
....

POST CODE .... PLANNED DISTANCE ....

TODAY'S WEATHER ....

TODAY'S TEMPERATURE .... START TIME ....

TODAY'S COMPANIONS ....

TODAY'S COMPANIONS ....

TODAY'S COMPANIONS ....

TODAY'S COMPANIONS ....

BREAKFAST ....

LUNCH ....

DINNER ....

WILDLIFE SEEN ....

END TIME .... TIME TAKEN ....

MILES COVERED .... DIFFICULTY 1 2 3 4 5

HIKE RATING ☆ ☆ ☆ ☆ ☆

TODAY'S HIGHLIGHTS

....
....
....
....

WALKING / HIKING NOTES

WALKING & HIKING IN IRELAND JOURNAL

TODAY'S DATE ..../ ..../ ....

START LOCATION GPS ....

START LOCATION / ADDRESS

....
....
....

POST CODE .... PLANNED DISTANCE...............

TODAY'S WEATHER ....

TODAY'S TEMPERATURE .... START TIME ....

TODAY'S COMPANIONS ....

TODAY'S COMPANIONS ....

TODAY'S COMPANIONS ....

TODAY'S COMPANIONS ....

BREAKFAST ....

LUNCH ....

DINNER ....

WILDLIFE SEEN ....

END TIME .... TIME TAKEN ....

MILES COVERED .... DIFFICULTY 1 2 3 4 5

HIKE RATING ☆ ☆ ☆ ☆ ☆

TODAY'S HIGHLIGHTS

....
....
....
....

WALKING / HIKING NOTES

WALKING & HIKING IN IRELAND JOURNAL

TODAY'S DATE .... / .... / ....

START LOCATION GPS ....

START LOCATION / ADDRESS

....
....
....

POST CODE .... PLANNED DISTANCE ....

TODAY'S WEATHER ....

TODAY'S TEMPERATURE .... START TIME ....

TODAY'S COMPANIONS ....

TODAY'S COMPANIONS ....

TODAY'S COMPANIONS ....

TODAY'S COMPANIONS ....

BREAKFAST ....

LUNCH ....

DINNER ....

WILDLIFE SEEN ....

END TIME .... TIME TAKEN ....

MILES COVERED .... DIFFICULTY 1 2 3 4 5

HIKE RATING ☆ ☆ ☆ ☆ ☆ ☆

TODAY'S HIGHLIGHTS

....
....
....
....

WALKING / HIKING NOTES

WALKING & HIKING IN IRELAND JOURNAL

TODAY'S DATE .... / ..../ ....

START LOCATION GPS ....

START LOCATION / ADDRESS

....
....
....

POST CODE .... PLANNED DISTANCE...............

TODAY'S WEATHER ....

TODAY'S TEMPERATURE .... START TIME ....

TODAY'S COMPANIONS ....

TODAY'S COMPANIONS ....

TODAY'S COMPANIONS ....

TODAY'S COMPANIONS ....

BREAKFAST ....

LUNCH ....

DINNER ....

WILDLIFE SEEN ....

END TIME .... TIME TAKEN ....

MILES COVERED .... DIFFICULTY 1 2 3 4 5

HIKE RATING ☆ ☆ ☆ ☆ ☆

TODAY'S HIGHLIGHTS

....
....
....
....

WALKING / HIKING NOTES

WALKING & HIKING IN IRELAND JOURNAL

TODAY'S DATE ..../ ..../ ....

START LOCATION GPS ....

START LOCATION / ADDRESS

....
....
....

POST CODE .... PLANNED DISTANCE...............

TODAY'S WEATHER ....

TODAY'S TEMPERATURE .... START TIME ....

TODAY'S COMPANIONS ....

TODAY'S COMPANIONS ....

TODAY'S COMPANIONS ....

TODAY'S COMPANIONS ....

BREAKFAST ....

LUNCH ....

DINNER ....

WILDLIFE SEEN ....

END TIME .... TIME TAKEN ....

MILES COVERED .... DIFFICULTY 1 2 3 4 5

HIKE RATING ☆ ☆ ☆ ☆ ☆

TODAY'S HIGHLIGHTS

....
....
....
....

WALKING / HIKING NOTES

WALKING & HIKING IN IRELAND JOURNAL

TODAY'S DATE .... / .... / ....

START LOCATION GPS ....

START LOCATION / ADDRESS

....
....
....

POST CODE .... PLANNED DISTANCE...............

TODAY'S WEATHER ....

TODAY'S TEMPERATURE .... START TIME ....

TODAY'S COMPANIONS ....

TODAY'S COMPANIONS ....

TODAY'S COMPANIONS ....

TODAY'S COMPANIONS ....

BREAKFAST ....

LUNCH ....

DINNER ....

WILDLIFE SEEN ....

END TIME .... TIME TAKEN ....

MILES COVERED .... DIFFICULTY 1 2 3 4 5

HIKE RATING ☆ ☆ ☆ ☆ ☆ ☆

TODAY'S HIGHLIGHTS

....
....
....
....

WALKING / HIKING NOTES

WALKING & HIKING IN IRELAND JOURNAL

TODAY'S DATE .... / .... / ....

START LOCATION GPS ....

START LOCATION / ADDRESS

....
....
....

POST CODE .... PLANNED DISTANCE...............
TODAY'S WEATHER ....
TODAY'S TEMPERATURE .... START TIME ....
TODAY'S COMPANIONS ....
TODAY'S COMPANIONS ....
TODAY'S COMPANIONS ....
TODAY'S COMPANIONS ....
BREAKFAST ....
LUNCH ....
DINNER ....
WILDLIFE SEEN ....
END TIME .... TIME TAKEN ....
MILES COVERED .... DIFFICULTY 1 2 3 4 5
HIKE RATING ☆ ☆ ☆ ☆ ☆

TODAY'S HIGHLIGHTS

....
....
....
....

WALKING / HIKING NOTES

WALKING & HIKING IN IRELAND JOURNAL

TODAY'S DATE ..... / ..... / ....

START LOCATION GPS ....

START LOCATION / ADDRESS

....
....
....

POST CODE .... PLANNED DISTANCE ....

TODAY'S WEATHER ....

TODAY'S TEMPERATURE .... START TIME ....

TODAY'S COMPANIONS ....

TODAY'S COMPANIONS ....

TODAY'S COMPANIONS ....

TODAY'S COMPANIONS ....

BREAKFAST ....

LUNCH ....

DINNER ....

WILDLIFE SEEN ....

END TIME .... TIME TAKEN ....

MILES COVERED .... DIFFICULTY 1 2 3 4 5

HIKE RATING ☆ ☆ ☆ ☆ ☆

TODAY'S HIGHLIGHTS

....
....
....
....

WALKING / HIKING NOTES

WALKING & HIKING IN IRELAND JOURNAL

TODAY'S DATE ..... / ..... / ....

START LOCATION GPS ....

START LOCATION / ADDRESS

....
....
....

POST CODE .... PLANNED DISTANCE ....

TODAY'S WEATHER ....

TODAY'S TEMPERATURE .... START TIME ....

TODAY'S COMPANIONS ....

TODAY'S COMPANIONS ....

TODAY'S COMPANIONS ....

TODAY'S COMPANIONS ....

BREAKFAST ....

LUNCH ....

DINNER ....

WILDLIFE SEEN ....

END TIME .... TIME TAKEN ....

MILES COVERED .... DIFFICULTY 1 2 3 4 5

HIKE RATING ☆ ☆ ☆ ☆ ☆ ☆

TODAY'S HIGHLIGHTS

....
....
....
....

WALKING / HIKING NOTES

WALKING & HIKING IN IRELAND JOURNAL

TODAY'S DATE .... / ..../ ....

START LOCATION GPS ....

START LOCATION / ADDRESS

....
....
....

POST CODE .... PLANNED DISTANCE...............

TODAY'S WEATHER ....

TODAY'S TEMPERATURE .... START TIME ....

TODAY'S COMPANIONS ....

TODAY'S COMPANIONS ....

TODAY'S COMPANIONS ....

TODAY'S COMPANIONS ....

BREAKFAST ....

LUNCH ....

DINNER ....

WILDLIFE SEEN ....

END TIME .... TIME TAKEN ....

MILES COVERED .... DIFFICULTY 1 2 3 4 5

HIKE RATING ☆ ☆ ☆ ☆ ☆ ☆

TODAY'S HIGHLIGHTS

....
....
....
....

WALKING / HIKING NOTES

WALKING & HIKING IN IRELAND JOURNAL

TODAY'S DATE ..../ ..../ ....

START LOCATION GPS ....

START LOCATION / ADDRESS

....
....
....

POST CODE .... PLANNED DISTANCE ....

TODAY'S WEATHER ....

TODAY'S TEMPERATURE .... START TIME ....

TODAY'S COMPANIONS ....

TODAY'S COMPANIONS ....

TODAY'S COMPANIONS ....

TODAY'S COMPANIONS ....

BREAKFAST ....

LUNCH ....

DINNER ....

WILDLIFE SEEN ....

END TIME .... TIME TAKEN ....

MILES COVERED .... DIFFICULTY 1 2 3 4 5

HIKE RATING ☆ ☆ ☆ ☆ ☆ ☆

TODAY'S HIGHLIGHTS

....
....
....
....

WALKING / HIKING NOTES

WALKING & HIKING IN IRELAND JOURNAL

TODAY'S DATE .... / .... / ....

START LOCATION GPS ....

START LOCATION / ADDRESS

....
....
....

POST CODE .... PLANNED DISTANCE ....

TODAY'S WEATHER ....

TODAY'S TEMPERATURE .... START TIME ....

TODAY'S COMPANIONS ....

TODAY'S COMPANIONS ....

TODAY'S COMPANIONS ....

TODAY'S COMPANIONS ....

BREAKFAST ....

LUNCH ....

DINNER ....

WILDLIFE SEEN ....

END TIME .... TIME TAKEN ....

MILES COVERED .... DIFFICULTY 1 2 3 4 5

HIKE RATING ☆ ☆ ☆ ☆ ☆ ☆

TODAY'S HIGHLIGHTS

....
....
....
....

WALKING / HIKING NOTES

WALKING & HIKING IN IRELAND JOURNAL

TODAY'S DATE .... / ..../ ....

START LOCATION GPS ....

START LOCATION / ADDRESS

....
....
....

POST CODE .... PLANNED DISTANCE...............
TODAY'S WEATHER ....
TODAY'S TEMPERATURE .... START TIME ....
TODAY'S COMPANIONS ....
TODAY'S COMPANIONS ....
TODAY'S COMPANIONS ....
TODAY'S COMPANIONS ....
BREAKFAST ....
LUNCH ....
DINNER ....
WILDLIFE SEEN ....
END TIME .... TIME TAKEN ....
MILES COVERED .... DIFFICULTY 1 2 3 4 5
HIKE RATING ☆ ☆ ☆ ☆ ☆ ☆

TODAY'S HIGHLIGHTS

....
....
....
....

WALKING / HIKING NOTES

WALKING & HIKING IN IRELAND JOURNAL

TODAY'S DATE ..../..../........

START LOCATION GPS ....

START LOCATION / ADDRESS

....
....
....

POST CODE .... PLANNED DISTANCE...............

TODAY'S WEATHER ....

TODAY'S TEMPERATURE .... START TIME ....

TODAY'S COMPANIONS ....

TODAY'S COMPANIONS ....

TODAY'S COMPANIONS ....

TODAY'S COMPANIONS ....

BREAKFAST ....

LUNCH ....

DINNER ....

WILDLIFE SEEN ....

END TIME .... TIME TAKEN ....

MILES COVERED .... DIFFICULTY 1   2   3   4   5

HIKE RATING   ☆ ☆ ☆ ☆ ☆

TODAY'S HIGHLIGHTS

....
....
....
....

WALKING / HIKING NOTES

WALKING & HIKING IN IRELAND JOURNAL

TODAY'S DATE ..... / ..... / ....

START LOCATION GPS ....

START LOCATION / ADDRESS

....
....
....

POST CODE .... PLANNED DISTANCE...............

TODAY'S WEATHER ....

TODAY'S TEMPERATURE .... START TIME ....

TODAY'S COMPANIONS ....

TODAY'S COMPANIONS ....

TODAY'S COMPANIONS ....

TODAY'S COMPANIONS ....

BREAKFAST ....

LUNCH ....

DINNER ....

WILDLIFE SEEN ....

END TIME .... TIME TAKEN ....

MILES COVERED .... DIFFICULTY 1   2   3   4   5

HIKE RATING   ☆ ☆ ☆ ☆ ☆ ☆

TODAY'S HIGHLIGHTS

....
....
....
....

WALKING / HIKING NOTES

WALKING & HIKING IN IRELAND JOURNAL

TODAY'S DATE ..../ ..../ ....

START LOCATION GPS ....

START LOCATION / ADDRESS

....
....
....

POST CODE .... PLANNED DISTANCE...............

TODAY'S WEATHER ....

TODAY'S TEMPERATURE .... START TIME ....

TODAY'S COMPANIONS ....

TODAY'S COMPANIONS ....

TODAY'S COMPANIONS ....

TODAY'S COMPANIONS ....

BREAKFAST ....

LUNCH ....

DINNER ....

WILDLIFE SEEN ....

END TIME .... TIME TAKEN ....

MILES COVERED .... DIFFICULTY 1 2 3 4 5

HIKE RATING ☆ ☆ ☆ ☆ ☆ ☆

TODAY'S HIGHLIGHTS

....
....
....
....

WALKING / HIKING NOTES

WALKING & HIKING IN IRELAND JOURNAL

TODAY'S DATE .... / .... / ....

START LOCATION GPS ....

START LOCATION / ADDRESS

....

....

....

POST CODE .... PLANNED DISTANCE ....

TODAY'S WEATHER ....

TODAY'S TEMPERATURE .... START TIME ....

TODAY'S COMPANIONS ....

TODAY'S COMPANIONS ....

TODAY'S COMPANIONS ....

TODAY'S COMPANIONS ....

BREAKFAST ....

LUNCH ....

DINNER ....

WILDLIFE SEEN ....

END TIME .... TIME TAKEN ....

MILES COVERED .... DIFFICULTY 1 2 3 4 5

HIKE RATING ☆ ☆ ☆ ☆ ☆

TODAY'S HIGHLIGHTS

....

....

....

....

WALKING / HIKING NOTES

WALKING & HIKING IN IRELAND JOURNAL

TODAY'S DATE .... / .... / ....

START LOCATION GPS ....

START LOCATION / ADDRESS

....
....
....

POST CODE .... PLANNED DISTANCE...............
TODAY'S WEATHER ....
TODAY'S TEMPERATURE .... START TIME ....
TODAY'S COMPANIONS ....
TODAY'S COMPANIONS ....
TODAY'S COMPANIONS ....
TODAY'S COMPANIONS ....
BREAKFAST ....
LUNCH ....
DINNER ....
WILDLIFE SEEN ....
END TIME .... TIME TAKEN ....
MILES COVERED .... DIFFICULTY 1 2 3 4 5
HIKE RATING ☆ ☆ ☆ ☆ ☆ ☆

TODAY'S HIGHLIGHTS

....
....
....
....

WALKING / HIKING NOTES

WALKING & HIKING IN IRELAND JOURNAL

TODAY'S DATE .... / .... / ....

START LOCATION GPS ....

START LOCATION / ADDRESS

....
....
....

POST CODE .... PLANNED DISTANCE...............
TODAY'S WEATHER ....
TODAY'S TEMPERATURE .... START TIME ....
TODAY'S COMPANIONS ....
TODAY'S COMPANIONS ....
TODAY'S COMPANIONS ....
TODAY'S COMPANIONS ....
BREAKFAST ....
LUNCH ....
DINNER ....
WILDLIFE SEEN ....
END TIME .... TIME TAKEN ....
MILES COVERED .... DIFFICULTY 1 2 3 4 5
HIKE RATING ☆ ☆ ☆ ☆ ☆

TODAY'S HIGHLIGHTS

....
....
....
....

WALKING / HIKING NOTES

WALKING & HIKING IN IRELAND JOURNAL

TODAY'S DATE ..../ ..../ ....

START LOCATION GPS ....

START LOCATION / ADDRESS

....
....
....

POST CODE .... PLANNED DISTANCE...............

TODAY'S WEATHER ....

TODAY'S TEMPERATURE .... START TIME ....

TODAY'S COMPANIONS ....

TODAY'S COMPANIONS ....

TODAY'S COMPANIONS ....

TODAY'S COMPANIONS ....

BREAKFAST ....

LUNCH ....

DINNER ....

WILDLIFE SEEN ....

END TIME .... TIME TAKEN ....

MILES COVERED .... DIFFICULTY 1   2   3   4   5

HIKE RATING ☆ ☆ ☆ ☆ ☆

TODAY'S HIGHLIGHTS

....
....
....
....

WALKING / HIKING NOTES

WALKING & HIKING IN IRELAND JOURNAL

TODAY'S DATE .... / ..../ ....

START LOCATION GPS ....

START LOCATION / ADDRESS

....
....
....

POST CODE .... PLANNED DISTANCE...............

TODAY'S WEATHER ....

TODAY'S TEMPERATURE .... START TIME ....

TODAY'S COMPANIONS ....

TODAY'S COMPANIONS ....

TODAY'S COMPANIONS ....

TODAY'S COMPANIONS ....

BREAKFAST ....

LUNCH ....

DINNER ....

WILDLIFE SEEN ....

END TIME .... TIME TAKEN ....

MILES COVERED .... DIFFICULTY 1 2 3 4 5

HIKE RATING ☆ ☆ ☆ ☆ ☆ ☆

TODAY'S HIGHLIGHTS

....
....
....
....

WALKING / HIKING NOTES

WALKING & HIKING IN IRELAND JOURNAL

TODAY'S DATE .... / ..../ ....

START LOCATION GPS ....

START LOCATION / ADDRESS

....
....
....

POST CODE .... PLANNED DISTANCE...............

TODAY'S WEATHER ....

TODAY'S TEMPERATURE .... START TIME ....

TODAY'S COMPANIONS ....

TODAY'S COMPANIONS ....

TODAY'S COMPANIONS ....

TODAY'S COMPANIONS ....

BREAKFAST ....

LUNCH ....

DINNER ....

WILDLIFE SEEN ....

END TIME .... TIME TAKEN ....

MILES COVERED .... DIFFICULTY 1 2 3 4 5

HIKE RATING ☆ ☆ ☆ ☆ ☆

TODAY'S HIGHLIGHTS

....
....
....
....

WALKING / HIKING NOTES

WALKING & HIKING IN IRELAND JOURNAL

TODAY'S DATE ..../ ..../ ....

START LOCATION GPS ....

START LOCATION / ADDRESS

....
....
....

POST CODE .... PLANNED DISTANCE...............

TODAY'S WEATHER ....

TODAY'S TEMPERATURE .... START TIME ....

TODAY'S COMPANIONS ....

TODAY'S COMPANIONS ....

TODAY'S COMPANIONS ....

TODAY'S COMPANIONS ....

BREAKFAST ....

LUNCH ....

DINNER ....

WILDLIFE SEEN ....

END TIME .... TIME TAKEN ....

MILES COVERED .... DIFFICULTY 1   2   3   4   5

HIKE RATING   ☆ ☆ ☆ ☆ ☆ ☆

TODAY'S HIGHLIGHTS

....
....
....
....

WALKING / HIKING NOTES

WALKING & HIKING IN IRELAND JOURNAL

TODAY'S DATE ..../ ..../ ....

START LOCATION GPS ....

START LOCATION / ADDRESS

....
....
....

POST CODE .... PLANNED DISTANCE..............

TODAY'S WEATHER ....

TODAY'S TEMPERATURE .... START TIME ....

TODAY'S COMPANIONS ....

TODAY'S COMPANIONS ....

TODAY'S COMPANIONS ....

TODAY'S COMPANIONS ....

BREAKFAST ....

LUNCH ....

DINNER ....

WILDLIFE SEEN ....

END TIME .... TIME TAKEN ....

MILES COVERED .... DIFFICULTY 1 2 3 4 5

HIKE RATING ☆ ☆ ☆ ☆ ☆ ☆

TODAY'S HIGHLIGHTS

....
....
....
....

WALKING / HIKING NOTES

WALKING & HIKING IN IRELAND JOURNAL

TODAY'S DATE ..... / ..... / ....

START LOCATION GPS ....

START LOCATION / ADDRESS

....
....
....

POST CODE .... PLANNED DISTANCE ....
TODAY'S WEATHER ....
TODAY'S TEMPERATURE .... START TIME ....
TODAY'S COMPANIONS ....
TODAY'S COMPANIONS ....
TODAY'S COMPANIONS ....
TODAY'S COMPANIONS ....
BREAKFAST ....
LUNCH ....
DINNER ....
WILDLIFE SEEN ....
END TIME .... TIME TAKEN ....
MILES COVERED .... DIFFICULTY 1 2 3 4 5
HIKE RATING   ☆ ☆ ☆ ☆ ☆ ☆

TODAY'S HIGHLIGHTS

....
....
....
....

WALKING / HIKING NOTES

WALKING & HIKING IN IRELAND JOURNAL

TODAY'S DATE ..... / ..... / ....

START LOCATION GPS ....

START LOCATION / ADDRESS

....
....
....

POST CODE .... PLANNED DISTANCE...............
TODAY'S WEATHER ....
TODAY'S TEMPERATURE .... START TIME ....
TODAY'S COMPANIONS ....
TODAY'S COMPANIONS ....
TODAY'S COMPANIONS ....
TODAY'S COMPANIONS ....
BREAKFAST ....
LUNCH ....
DINNER ....
WILDLIFE SEEN ....
END TIME .... TIME TAKEN ....
MILES COVERED .... DIFFICULTY 1 2 3 4 5
HIKE RATING ☆ ☆ ☆ ☆ ☆

TODAY'S HIGHLIGHTS

....
....
....
....

WALKING / HIKING NOTES

WALKING & HIKING IN IRELAND JOURNAL

TODAY'S DATE ..... / ..... / ....

START LOCATION GPS ....

START LOCATION / ADDRESS

....
....
....

POST CODE .... PLANNED DISTANCE ....

TODAY'S WEATHER ....

TODAY'S TEMPERATURE .... START TIME ....

TODAY'S COMPANIONS ....

TODAY'S COMPANIONS ....

TODAY'S COMPANIONS ....

TODAY'S COMPANIONS ....

BREAKFAST ....

LUNCH ....

DINNER ....

WILDLIFE SEEN ....

END TIME .... TIME TAKEN ....

MILES COVERED .... DIFFICULTY 1 2 3 4 5

HIKE RATING ☆ ☆ ☆ ☆ ☆ ☆

TODAY'S HIGHLIGHTS

....
....
....
....

WALKING / HIKING NOTES

WALKING & HIKING IN IRELAND JOURNAL

TODAY'S DATE ..... / ..... / ....

START LOCATION GPS ....

START LOCATION / ADDRESS

....
....
....

POST CODE .... PLANNED DISTANCE ....
TODAY'S WEATHER ....
TODAY'S TEMPERATURE .... START TIME ....
TODAY'S COMPANIONS ....
TODAY'S COMPANIONS ....
TODAY'S COMPANIONS ....
TODAY'S COMPANIONS ....
BREAKFAST ....
LUNCH ....
DINNER ....
WILDLIFE SEEN ....
END TIME .... TIME TAKEN ....
MILES COVERED .... DIFFICULTY 1 2 3 4 5
HIKE RATING ☆ ☆ ☆ ☆ ☆ ☆

TODAY'S HIGHLIGHTS

....
....
....
....

WALKING / HIKING NOTES

WALKING & HIKING IN IRELAND JOURNAL

TODAY'S DATE .... / .... / ....

START LOCATION GPS ....

START LOCATION / ADDRESS

....
....
....

POST CODE .... PLANNED DISTANCE...............

TODAY'S WEATHER ....

TODAY'S TEMPERATURE .... START TIME ....

TODAY'S COMPANIONS ....

TODAY'S COMPANIONS ....

TODAY'S COMPANIONS ....

TODAY'S COMPANIONS ....

BREAKFAST ....

LUNCH ....

DINNER ....

WILDLIFE SEEN ....

END TIME .... TIME TAKEN ....

MILES COVERED .... DIFFICULTY 1 2 3 4 5

HIKE RATING ☆ ☆ ☆ ☆ ☆

TODAY'S HIGHLIGHTS

....
....
....
....

WALKING / HIKING NOTES

WALKING & HIKING IN IRELAND JOURNAL

TODAY'S DATE ..... / ..... / ....

START LOCATION GPS ....

START LOCATION / ADDRESS

....
....
....

POST CODE .... PLANNED DISTANCE...............

TODAY'S WEATHER ....

TODAY'S TEMPERATURE .... START TIME ....

TODAY'S COMPANIONS ....

TODAY'S COMPANIONS ....

TODAY'S COMPANIONS ....

TODAY'S COMPANIONS ....

BREAKFAST ....

LUNCH ....

DINNER ....

WILDLIFE SEEN ....

END TIME .... TIME TAKEN ....

MILES COVERED .... DIFFICULTY 1 2 3 4 5

HIKE RATING ☆ ☆ ☆ ☆ ☆ ☆

TODAY'S HIGHLIGHTS

....
....
....
....

WALKING / HIKING NOTES

WALKING & HIKING IN IRELAND JOURNAL

TODAY'S DATE .... / ..../ ....

START LOCATION GPS ....

START LOCATION / ADDRESS

....
....
....

POST CODE .... PLANNED DISTANCE...............
TODAY'S WEATHER ....
TODAY'S TEMPERATURE .... START TIME ....
TODAY'S COMPANIONS ....
TODAY'S COMPANIONS ....
TODAY'S COMPANIONS ....
TODAY'S COMPANIONS ....
BREAKFAST ....
LUNCH ....
DINNER ....
WILDLIFE SEEN ....
END TIME .... TIME TAKEN ....
MILES COVERED .... DIFFICULTY 1 2 3 4 5
HIKE RATING ☆ ☆ ☆ ☆ ☆

TODAY'S HIGHLIGHTS

....
....
....
....

WALKING / HIKING NOTES

WALKING & HIKING IN IRELAND JOURNAL

TODAY'S DATE ..... / ...../ ....

START LOCATION GPS ....

START LOCATION / ADDRESS

....
....
....

POST CODE .... PLANNED DISTANCE...............

TODAY'S WEATHER ....

TODAY'S TEMPERATURE .... START TIME ....

TODAY'S COMPANIONS ....

TODAY'S COMPANIONS ....

TODAY'S COMPANIONS ....

TODAY'S COMPANIONS ....

BREAKFAST ....

LUNCH ....

DINNER ....

WILDLIFE SEEN ....

END TIME .... TIME TAKEN ....

MILES COVERED .... DIFFICULTY 1 2 3 4 5

HIKE RATING   ☆ ☆ ☆ ☆ ☆

TODAY'S HIGHLIGHTS

....
....
....
....

WALKING / HIKING NOTES

WALKING & HIKING IN IRELAND JOURNAL

TODAY'S DATE .... / ..../ ....

START LOCATION GPS ....

START LOCATION / ADDRESS

....
....
....

POST CODE .... PLANNED DISTANCE...............
TODAY'S WEATHER ....
TODAY'S TEMPERATURE .... START TIME ....
TODAY'S COMPANIONS ....
TODAY'S COMPANIONS ....
TODAY'S COMPANIONS ....
TODAY'S COMPANIONS ....
BREAKFAST ....
LUNCH ....
DINNER ....
WILDLIFE SEEN ....
END TIME .... TIME TAKEN ....
MILES COVERED .... DIFFICULTY 1 2 3 4 5
HIKE RATING ☆ ☆ ☆ ☆ ☆ ☆

TODAY'S HIGHLIGHTS

....
....
....
....

WALKING / HIKING NOTES

WALKING & HIKING IN IRELAND JOURNAL

TODAY'S DATE .... / ..../ ....

START LOCATION GPS ....

START LOCATION / ADDRESS

....
....
....

POST CODE .... PLANNED DISTANCE...............
TODAY'S WEATHER ....
TODAY'S TEMPERATURE .... START TIME ....
TODAY'S COMPANIONS ....
TODAY'S COMPANIONS ....
TODAY'S COMPANIONS ....
TODAY'S COMPANIONS ....
BREAKFAST ....
LUNCH ....
DINNER ....
WILDLIFE SEEN ....
END TIME .... TIME TAKEN ....
MILES COVERED .... DIFFICULTY 1 2 3 4 5
HIKE RATING ☆ ☆ ☆ ☆ ☆

TODAY'S HIGHLIGHTS

....
....
....
....

WALKING / HIKING NOTES

WALKING & HIKING IN IRELAND JOURNAL

TODAY'S DATE .... / .... / ....

START LOCATION GPS ....

START LOCATION / ADDRESS

....
....
....

POST CODE .... PLANNED DISTANCE...............

TODAY'S WEATHER ....

TODAY'S TEMPERATURE .... START TIME ....

TODAY'S COMPANIONS ....

TODAY'S COMPANIONS ....

TODAY'S COMPANIONS ....

TODAY'S COMPANIONS ....

BREAKFAST ....

LUNCH ....

DINNER ....

WILDLIFE SEEN ....

END TIME .... TIME TAKEN ....

MILES COVERED .... DIFFICULTY 1 2 3 4 5

HIKE RATING ☆ ☆ ☆ ☆ ☆

TODAY'S HIGHLIGHTS

....
....
....
....

WALKING / HIKING NOTES

WALKING & HIKING IN IRELAND JOURNAL

TODAY'S DATE ..... / ..... / ....

START LOCATION GPS ....

START LOCATION / ADDRESS

....
....
....

POST CODE .... PLANNED DISTANCE...............

TODAY'S WEATHER ....

TODAY'S TEMPERATURE .... START TIME ....

TODAY'S COMPANIONS ....

TODAY'S COMPANIONS ....

TODAY'S COMPANIONS ....

TODAY'S COMPANIONS ....

BREAKFAST ....

LUNCH ....

DINNER ....

WILDLIFE SEEN ....

END TIME .... TIME TAKEN ....

MILES COVERED .... DIFFICULTY 1   2   3   4   5

HIKE RATING ☆ ☆ ☆ ☆ ☆ ☆

TODAY'S HIGHLIGHTS

....
....
....
....

WALKING / HIKING NOTES

WALKING & HIKING IN IRELAND JOURNAL

TODAY'S DATE ..... / ..... / ....

START LOCATION GPS ....

START LOCATION / ADDRESS

....
....
....

POST CODE .... PLANNED DISTANCE...............

TODAY'S WEATHER ....

TODAY'S TEMPERATURE .... START TIME ....

TODAY'S COMPANIONS ....

TODAY'S COMPANIONS ....

TODAY'S COMPANIONS ....

TODAY'S COMPANIONS ....

BREAKFAST ....

LUNCH ....

DINNER ....

WILDLIFE SEEN ....

END TIME .... TIME TAKEN ....

MILES COVERED .... DIFFICULTY 1 2 3 4 5

HIKE RATING ☆ ☆ ☆ ☆ ☆ ☆

TODAY'S HIGHLIGHTS

....
....
....
....

WALKING / HIKING NOTES

WALKING & HIKING IN IRELAND JOURNAL

TODAY'S DATE ..../ ..../ ....

START LOCATION GPS ....

START LOCATION / ADDRESS

....
....
....

POST CODE .... PLANNED DISTANCE...............

TODAY'S WEATHER ....

TODAY'S TEMPERATURE .... START TIME ....

TODAY'S COMPANIONS ....

TODAY'S COMPANIONS ....

TODAY'S COMPANIONS ....

TODAY'S COMPANIONS ....

BREAKFAST ....

LUNCH ....

DINNER ....

WILDLIFE SEEN ....

END TIME .... TIME TAKEN ....

MILES COVERED .... DIFFICULTY 1 2 3 4 5

HIKE RATING ☆ ☆ ☆ ☆ ☆

TODAY'S HIGHLIGHTS

....
....
....
....

WALKING / HIKING NOTES

WALKING & HIKING IN IRELAND JOURNAL

TODAY'S DATE .... / .... / ....

START LOCATION GPS ....

START LOCATION / ADDRESS

....
....
....

POST CODE .... PLANNED DISTANCE ....
TODAY'S WEATHER ....
TODAY'S TEMPERATURE .... START TIME ....
TODAY'S COMPANIONS ....
TODAY'S COMPANIONS ....
TODAY'S COMPANIONS ....
TODAY'S COMPANIONS ....
BREAKFAST ....
LUNCH ....
DINNER ....
WILDLIFE SEEN ....
END TIME .... TIME TAKEN ....
MILES COVERED .... DIFFICULTY 1 2 3 4 5
HIKE RATING ☆ ☆ ☆ ☆ ☆ ☆

TODAY'S HIGHLIGHTS

....
....
....
....

WALKING / HIKING NOTES

WALKING & HIKING IN IRELAND JOURNAL

TODAY'S DATE .... / .... / ....

START LOCATION GPS ....

START LOCATION / ADDRESS

....
....
....

POST CODE .... PLANNED DISTANCE...............
TODAY'S WEATHER ....
TODAY'S TEMPERATURE .... START TIME ....
TODAY'S COMPANIONS ....
TODAY'S COMPANIONS ....
TODAY'S COMPANIONS ....
TODAY'S COMPANIONS ....
BREAKFAST ....
LUNCH ....
DINNER ....
WILDLIFE SEEN ....
END TIME .... TIME TAKEN ....
MILES COVERED .... DIFFICULTY 1 2 3 4 5
HIKE RATING ☆ ☆ ☆ ☆ ☆

TODAY'S HIGHLIGHTS

....
....
....
....

WALKING / HIKING NOTES

WALKING & HIKING IN IRELAND JOURNAL

TODAY'S DATE .... / .... / ....

START LOCATION GPS ....

START LOCATION / ADDRESS

....
....
....

POST CODE .... PLANNED DISTANCE...............
TODAY'S WEATHER ....
TODAY'S TEMPERATURE .... START TIME ....
TODAY'S COMPANIONS ....
TODAY'S COMPANIONS ....
TODAY'S COMPANIONS ....
TODAY'S COMPANIONS ....
BREAKFAST ....
LUNCH ....
DINNER ....
WILDLIFE SEEN ....
END TIME .... TIME TAKEN ....
MILES COVERED .... DIFFICULTY 1 2 3 4 5
HIKE RATING ☆ ☆ ☆ ☆ ☆

TODAY'S HIGHLIGHTS

....
....
....
....

WALKING / HIKING NOTES

WALKING & HIKING IN IRELAND JOURNAL

TODAY'S DATE .... / .... / ....

START LOCATION GPS ....

START LOCATION / ADDRESS

....
....
....

POST CODE .... PLANNED DISTANCE ....

TODAY'S WEATHER ....

TODAY'S TEMPERATURE .... START TIME ....

TODAY'S COMPANIONS ....

TODAY'S COMPANIONS ....

TODAY'S COMPANIONS ....

TODAY'S COMPANIONS ....

BREAKFAST ....

LUNCH ....

DINNER ....

WILDLIFE SEEN ....

END TIME .... TIME TAKEN ....

MILES COVERED .... DIFFICULTY 1 2 3 4 5

HIKE RATING ☆ ☆ ☆ ☆ ☆ ☆

TODAY'S HIGHLIGHTS

....
....
....
....

WALKING / HIKING NOTES

WALKING & HIKING IN IRELAND JOURNAL

TODAY'S DATE ..../ ..../ ....

START LOCATION GPS ....

START LOCATION / ADDRESS

....
....
....

POST CODE .... PLANNED DISTANCE ....
TODAY'S WEATHER ....
TODAY'S TEMPERATURE .... START TIME ....
TODAY'S COMPANIONS ....
TODAY'S COMPANIONS ....
TODAY'S COMPANIONS ....
TODAY'S COMPANIONS ....
BREAKFAST ....
LUNCH ....
DINNER ....
WILDLIFE SEEN ....
END TIME .... TIME TAKEN ....
MILES COVERED .... DIFFICULTY 1 2 3 4 5
HIKE RATING ☆ ☆ ☆ ☆ ☆ ☆

TODAY'S HIGHLIGHTS

....
....
....
....

WALKING / HIKING NOTES

WALKING & HIKING IN IRELAND JOURNAL

TODAY'S DATE ..... / ..... / ....

START LOCATION GPS ....

START LOCATION / ADDRESS

....
....
....

POST CODE .... PLANNED DISTANCE ....

TODAY'S WEATHER ....

TODAY'S TEMPERATURE .... START TIME ....

TODAY'S COMPANIONS ....

TODAY'S COMPANIONS ....

TODAY'S COMPANIONS ....

TODAY'S COMPANIONS ....

BREAKFAST ....

LUNCH ....

DINNER ....

WILDLIFE SEEN ....

END TIME .... TIME TAKEN ....

MILES COVERED .... DIFFICULTY 1 2 3 4 5

HIKE RATING ☆ ☆ ☆ ☆ ☆

TODAY'S HIGHLIGHTS

....
....
....
....

WALKING / HIKING NOTES

WALKING & HIKING IN IRELAND JOURNAL

TODAY'S DATE ..../..../........

START LOCATION GPS ....

START LOCATION / ADDRESS

....
....
....

POST CODE .... PLANNED DISTANCE...............

TODAY'S WEATHER ....

TODAY'S TEMPERATURE .... START TIME ....

TODAY'S COMPANIONS ....

TODAY'S COMPANIONS ....

TODAY'S COMPANIONS ....

TODAY'S COMPANIONS ....

BREAKFAST ....

LUNCH ....

DINNER ....

WILDLIFE SEEN ....

END TIME .... TIME TAKEN ....

MILES COVERED .... DIFFICULTY 1 2 3 4 5

HIKE RATING ☆ ☆ ☆ ☆ ☆ ☆

TODAY'S HIGHLIGHTS

....
....
....
....

WALKING / HIKING NOTES

WALKING & HIKING IN IRELAND JOURNAL

TODAY'S DATE .... / ..../ ....

START LOCATION GPS ....

START LOCATION / ADDRESS

....
....
....

POST CODE .... PLANNED DISTANCE...............
TODAY'S WEATHER ....
TODAY'S TEMPERATURE .... START TIME ....
TODAY'S COMPANIONS ....
TODAY'S COMPANIONS ....
TODAY'S COMPANIONS ....
TODAY'S COMPANIONS ....
BREAKFAST ....
LUNCH ....
DINNER ....
WILDLIFE SEEN ....
END TIME .... TIME TAKEN ....
MILES COVERED .... DIFFICULTY 1   2   3   4   5
HIKE RATING   ☆ ☆ ☆ ☆ ☆

TODAY'S HIGHLIGHTS

....
....
....
....

WALKING / HIKING NOTES

WALKING & HIKING IN IRELAND JOURNAL

TODAY'S DATE .... / .... / ....

START LOCATION GPS ....

START LOCATION / ADDRESS

....
....
....

POST CODE .... PLANNED DISTANCE...............
TODAY'S WEATHER ....
TODAY'S TEMPERATURE .... START TIME ....
TODAY'S COMPANIONS ....
TODAY'S COMPANIONS ....
TODAY'S COMPANIONS ....
TODAY'S COMPANIONS ....
BREAKFAST ....
LUNCH ....
DINNER ....
WILDLIFE SEEN ....
END TIME .... TIME TAKEN ....
MILES COVERED .... DIFFICULTY 1 2 3 4 5
HIKE RATING ☆ ☆ ☆ ☆ ☆

TODAY'S HIGHLIGHTS

....
....
....
....

WALKING / HIKING NOTES

WALKING & HIKING IN IRELAND JOURNAL

TODAY'S DATE ..../ ..../ ....

START LOCATION GPS ....

START LOCATION / ADDRESS

....
....
....

POST CODE .... PLANNED DISTANCE...............
TODAY'S WEATHER ....
TODAY'S TEMPERATURE .... START TIME ....
TODAY'S COMPANIONS ....
TODAY'S COMPANIONS ....
TODAY'S COMPANIONS ....
TODAY'S COMPANIONS ....
BREAKFAST ....
LUNCH ....
DINNER ....
WILDLIFE SEEN ....
END TIME .... TIME TAKEN ....
MILES COVERED .... DIFFICULTY 1 2 3 4 5
HIKE RATING ☆ ☆ ☆ ☆ ☆ ☆

TODAY'S HIGHLIGHTS

....
....
....
....

WALKING / HIKING NOTES

WALKING & HIKING IN IRELAND JOURNAL

TODAY'S DATE …. / …./ ……..

START LOCATION GPS ………………………………………………………

START LOCATION / ADDRESS

………………………………………………………………………………
………………………………………………………………………………
………………………………………………………………………………

POST CODE ………………… PLANNED DISTANCE……………

TODAY'S WEATHER ……………………………………………………

TODAY'S TEMPERATURE …………… START TIME ……………

TODAY'S COMPANIONS …………………………………………………

TODAY'S COMPANIONS …………………………………………………

TODAY'S COMPANIONS …………………………………………………

TODAY'S COMPANIONS …………………………………………………

BREAKFAST ………………………………………………………………

LUNCH ……………………………………………………………………

DINNER ……………………………………………………………………

WILDLIFE SEEN …………………………………………………………

END TIME ………………… TIME TAKEN …………………………

MILES COVERED …………… DIFFICULTY 1 2 3 4 5

HIKE RATING ☆ ☆ ☆ ☆ ☆ ☆

TODAY'S HIGHLIGHTS

………………………………………………………………………………
………………………………………………………………………………
………………………………………………………………………………
………………………………………………………………………………

WALKING / HIKING NOTES

WALKING & HIKING IN IRELAND JOURNAL

TODAY'S DATE ..../..../........

START LOCATION GPS ....

START LOCATION / ADDRESS

....
....
....

POST CODE .... PLANNED DISTANCE...............
TODAY'S WEATHER ....
TODAY'S TEMPERATURE .... START TIME ....
TODAY'S COMPANIONS ....
TODAY'S COMPANIONS ....
TODAY'S COMPANIONS ....
TODAY'S COMPANIONS ....
BREAKFAST ....
LUNCH ....
DINNER ....
WILDLIFE SEEN ....
END TIME .... TIME TAKEN ....
MILES COVERED .... DIFFICULTY 1 2 3 4 5
HIKE RATING ☆ ☆ ☆ ☆ ☆

TODAY'S HIGHLIGHTS

....
....
....
....

WALKING / HIKING NOTES

WALKING & HIKING IN IRELAND JOURNAL

TODAY'S DATE .... / ..../ ....

START LOCATION GPS ....

START LOCATION / ADDRESS

....
....
....

POST CODE .... PLANNED DISTANCE..............
TODAY'S WEATHER ....
TODAY'S TEMPERATURE .... START TIME ....
TODAY'S COMPANIONS ....
TODAY'S COMPANIONS ....
TODAY'S COMPANIONS ....
TODAY'S COMPANIONS ....
BREAKFAST ....
LUNCH ....
DINNER ....
WILDLIFE SEEN ....
END TIME .... TIME TAKEN ....
MILES COVERED .... DIFFICULTY 1 2 3 4 5
HIKE RATING ☆ ☆ ☆ ☆ ☆ ☆

TODAY'S HIGHLIGHTS

....
....
....
....

WALKING / HIKING NOTES

WALKING & HIKING IN IRELAND JOURNAL

TODAY'S DATE ..../ ..../ ....

START LOCATION GPS ....

START LOCATION / ADDRESS

....
....
....

POST CODE .... PLANNED DISTANCE...............
TODAY'S WEATHER ....
TODAY'S TEMPERATURE .... START TIME ....
TODAY'S COMPANIONS ....
TODAY'S COMPANIONS ....
TODAY'S COMPANIONS ....
TODAY'S COMPANIONS ....
BREAKFAST ....
LUNCH ....
DINNER ....
WILDLIFE SEEN ....
END TIME .... TIME TAKEN ....
MILES COVERED .... DIFFICULTY 1 2 3 4 5
HIKE RATING ☆ ☆ ☆ ☆ ☆

TODAY'S HIGHLIGHTS

....
....
....
....

WALKING / HIKING NOTES

WALKING & HIKING IN IRELAND JOURNAL

TODAY'S DATE .... / .... / ....

START LOCATION GPS ....

START LOCATION / ADDRESS

....

....

....

POST CODE .... PLANNED DISTANCE...............

TODAY'S WEATHER ....

TODAY'S TEMPERATURE .... START TIME ....

TODAY'S COMPANIONS ....

TODAY'S COMPANIONS ....

TODAY'S COMPANIONS ....

TODAY'S COMPANIONS ....

BREAKFAST ....

LUNCH ....

DINNER ....

WILDLIFE SEEN ....

END TIME .... TIME TAKEN ....

MILES COVERED .... DIFFICULTY 1 2 3 4 5

HIKE RATING ☆ ☆ ☆ ☆ ☆

TODAY'S HIGHLIGHTS

....

....

....

....

WALKING / HIKING NOTES

WALKING & HIKING IN IRELAND JOURNAL

TODAY'S DATE .... / .... / ....

START LOCATION GPS ....

START LOCATION / ADDRESS

....
....
....

POST CODE .... PLANNED DISTANCE...............

TODAY'S WEATHER ....

TODAY'S TEMPERATURE .... START TIME ....

TODAY'S COMPANIONS ....

TODAY'S COMPANIONS ....

TODAY'S COMPANIONS ....

TODAY'S COMPANIONS ....

BREAKFAST ....

LUNCH ....

DINNER ....

WILDLIFE SEEN ....

END TIME .... TIME TAKEN ....

MILES COVERED .... DIFFICULTY 1 2 3 4 5

HIKE RATING   ☆ ☆ ☆ ☆ ☆ ☆

TODAY'S HIGHLIGHTS

....
....
....
....

WALKING / HIKING NOTES

WALKING & HIKING IN IRELAND JOURNAL

TODAY'S DATE .... / ..../ ....

START LOCATION GPS ....

START LOCATION / ADDRESS

....
....
....

POST CODE .... PLANNED DISTANCE...............
TODAY'S WEATHER ....
TODAY'S TEMPERATURE .... START TIME ....
TODAY'S COMPANIONS ....
TODAY'S COMPANIONS ....
TODAY'S COMPANIONS ....
TODAY'S COMPANIONS ....
BREAKFAST ....
LUNCH ....
DINNER ....
WILDLIFE SEEN ....
END TIME .... TIME TAKEN ....
MILES COVERED .... DIFFICULTY 1 2 3 4 5
HIKE RATING ☆ ☆ ☆ ☆ ☆ ☆

TODAY'S HIGHLIGHTS

....
....
....
....

WALKING / HIKING NOTES

WALKING & HIKING IN IRELAND JOURNAL

TODAY'S DATE ..../..../........

START LOCATION GPS ....

START LOCATION / ADDRESS

....
....
....

POST CODE .... PLANNED DISTANCE...............
TODAY'S WEATHER ....
TODAY'S TEMPERATURE .... START TIME ....
TODAY'S COMPANIONS ....
TODAY'S COMPANIONS ....
TODAY'S COMPANIONS ....
TODAY'S COMPANIONS ....
BREAKFAST ....
LUNCH ....
DINNER ....
WILDLIFE SEEN ....
END TIME .... TIME TAKEN ....
MILES COVERED .... DIFFICULTY   1   2   3   4   5
HIKE RATING   ☆ ☆ ☆ ☆ ☆

TODAY'S HIGHLIGHTS

....
....
....
....

WALKING / HIKING NOTES

Printed in Great Britain
by Amazon